HEROIC JOBS

T0084891

FIGHTING CRIME

Revised Edition

Ellen Labrecque

Heinemann
LIBRARY
Chicago, Illinois

www.capstonepub.com
Visit our website to find out more information about Heinemann-Raintree books.

To order:

Phone 800-747-4992
Visit www.capstonepub.com to browse our catalog and order online.

© 2012 Heinemann Library
an imprint of Capstone Global Library, LLC
Chicago, Illinois

All rights reserved. No part of this publication may be reproduced or transmitted in any form or by any means, electronic or mechanical, including photocopying, recording, taping, or any information storage and retrieval system, without permission in writing from the publisher.

Edited by Dan Nunn, Rebecca Rissman, and Catherine Veitch
Designed by Joanne Malivoire
Picture research by Elizabeth Alexander
Originated by Capstone Global Library

Library of Congress Cataloging-in-Publication Data
Labrecque, Ellen.
Fighting crime / Ellen Labrecque.
p. cm.—(Heroic jobs)
Includes bibliographical references and index.
ISBN 978-1-4109-9827-9 (pb)—ISBN 978-1-4109-9824-8 (ebook pdf) 1. Police—Juvenile literature. 2. Police—Special weapons and tactics units—Juvenile literature. 3. Raids (Military science)—Juvenile literature. I. Title.
HV7922.L23 2012
363.2'32—dc22 2011015810

Acknowledgments
We would like to thank the following for permission to reproduce photographs: Alamy: Altered Images, 14, ENRIQUE MARCARIAN/Reuters, 21, imageBROKER, cover, 8, Jeffrey Isaac Greenberg 15+, 19, JHB Photography, 26, Les Gibbon, 5, 6, 17, Michael Matthews, Police Images, 22, 16; Getty Images: ANTONIO SCORZA, 18, ATTILA KISBENEDEK, 4, Chris Jackson, 9, EVARISTO SA/AFP, 15, Handout, 7, Image Source, 11, moodboard, 13, NICOLAS MAETERLINCK/AFP, 12; iStockphoto: Terraxplorer, 28; Newscom: Post Staff Photographer/SCMP, 20; Shutterstock Premier: Daniel Graves, 29, Nils Jorgensen, 23; Shutterstock: Fractal Pictures, 25, Gorgev, 24, Mr.Nino, 27, Peter Kim, 10

Every effort has been made to contact copyright holders of material reproduced in this book. Any omissions will be rectified in subsequent printings if notice is given to the publisher.

Disclaimer
All the Internet addresses (URLs) given in this book were valid at the time of going to press. However, due to the dynamic nature of the Internet, some addresses may have changed, or sites may have changed or ceased to exist since publication. While the author and Publishers regret any inconvenience this may cause readers, no responsibility for any such changes can be accepted by either the author or the Publishers.

Some words are shown in bold, **like this**. You can find out what they mean by looking in the glossary.

Printed in the United States 4384

Contents

Action! 4
What Is a Police Raid? 6
Who Are the Police? 8
The Investigation 10
Teamwork Works 12
Danger! 14
Equipment 16
Catching Drug Dealers 18
Stolen Goods 20
Escape! 22
Caught in the Act 24
Becoming a Police Officer 26
Stay Safe 28
Glossary *30*
Find Out More *31*
Index *32*

Action!

The time is 5:00 a.m. Most people are asleep, except police officers on a raid. The officers surround the house of a suspected criminal. They knock loudly on the door and shout to be let in. When nobody answers, the officers break the door down and charge in.

POLICE
452

What Is a Police Raid?

A police raid is when police officers surprise **suspects** and **arrest** them, or search for **evidence**. Suspects are people that the police think are guilty of a crime. Raids are used when police think the suspects will **resist**, or fight against, the arrest.

Did you know?
Police raids that take place in the early morning are also called "dawn raids."

Who Are the Police?

Police officers are in charge of keeping order in their local area. Officers stop, or **prevent**, crime from happening. They also discover, or **detect**, crime. They must be smart and honest. They must also be very fit.

Police officers also need to be brave.

The Investigation

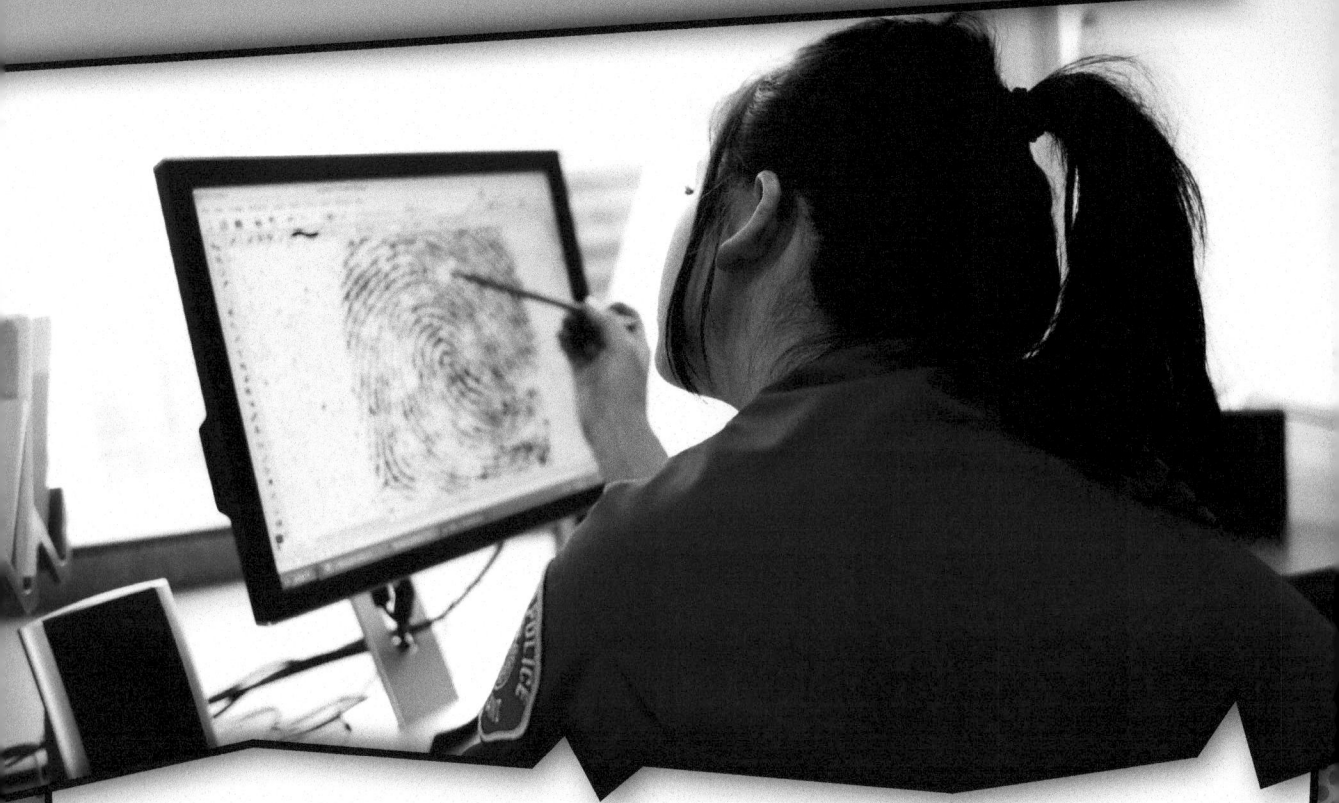

Police **investigate**, or research facts about a crime, before making a raid. During an investigation, police officers collect **evidence** to prove what has happened. They also **interrogate** people who may have seen what happened. These people are called **witnesses**.

CITY OF NEW YORK
POLICE

Teamwork Works

Each member of the police raid team has a job. Some officers look for **evidence** at the scene of the crime. Other officers are **lookouts**. Lookouts watch to make sure the **suspect** doesn't escape. They also keep people away from the crime scene.

Dogs are part of the team, too!

Danger!

Raids can be dangerous. Police never know for certain what they will find. There could be more **suspects** than they first thought. There could also be explosives, such as bombs, or loaded guns. The more prepared the police are, the safer they will be.

All of these weapons were seized in a police raid in November 2010, in Rio de Janeiro, Brazil.

Equipment

Each police officer wears about 35 pounds of equipment on a raid. The equipment includes a bulletproof vest to protect against getting hurt, firearms, a radio, and handcuffs to **arrest** the **suspects**.

Did you know?
A police officer may use a taser gun to fire an electric shock at a suspect if the suspect is threatening the officer with violence. Usually, a taser gun does no long-term harm.

Catching Drug Dealers

Drug dealers are criminals who sell drugs **illegally**. These drugs can make the people who take them very ill or even kill them. The police try to stop people from selling drugs illegally.

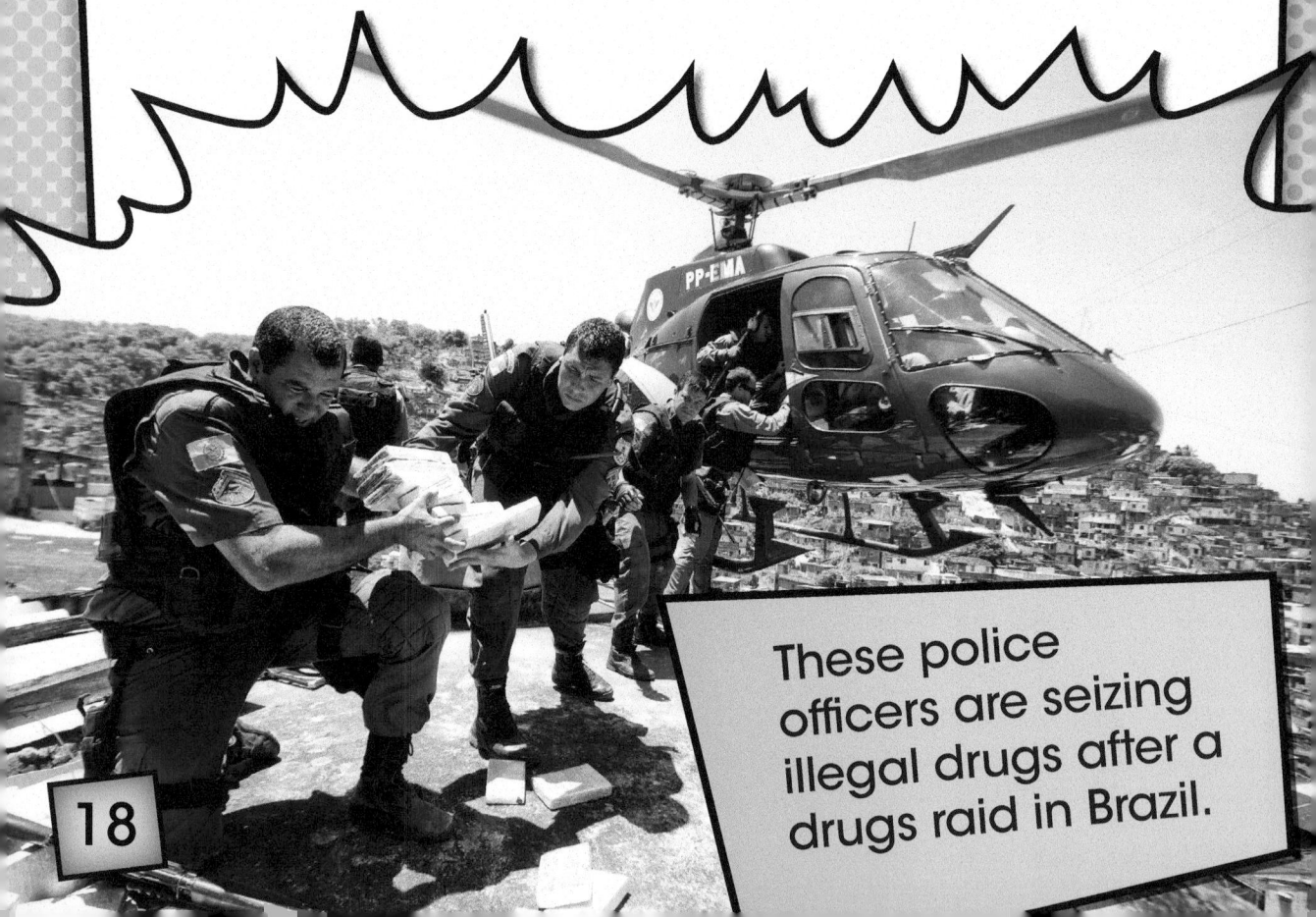

These police officers are seizing illegal drugs after a drugs raid in Brazil.

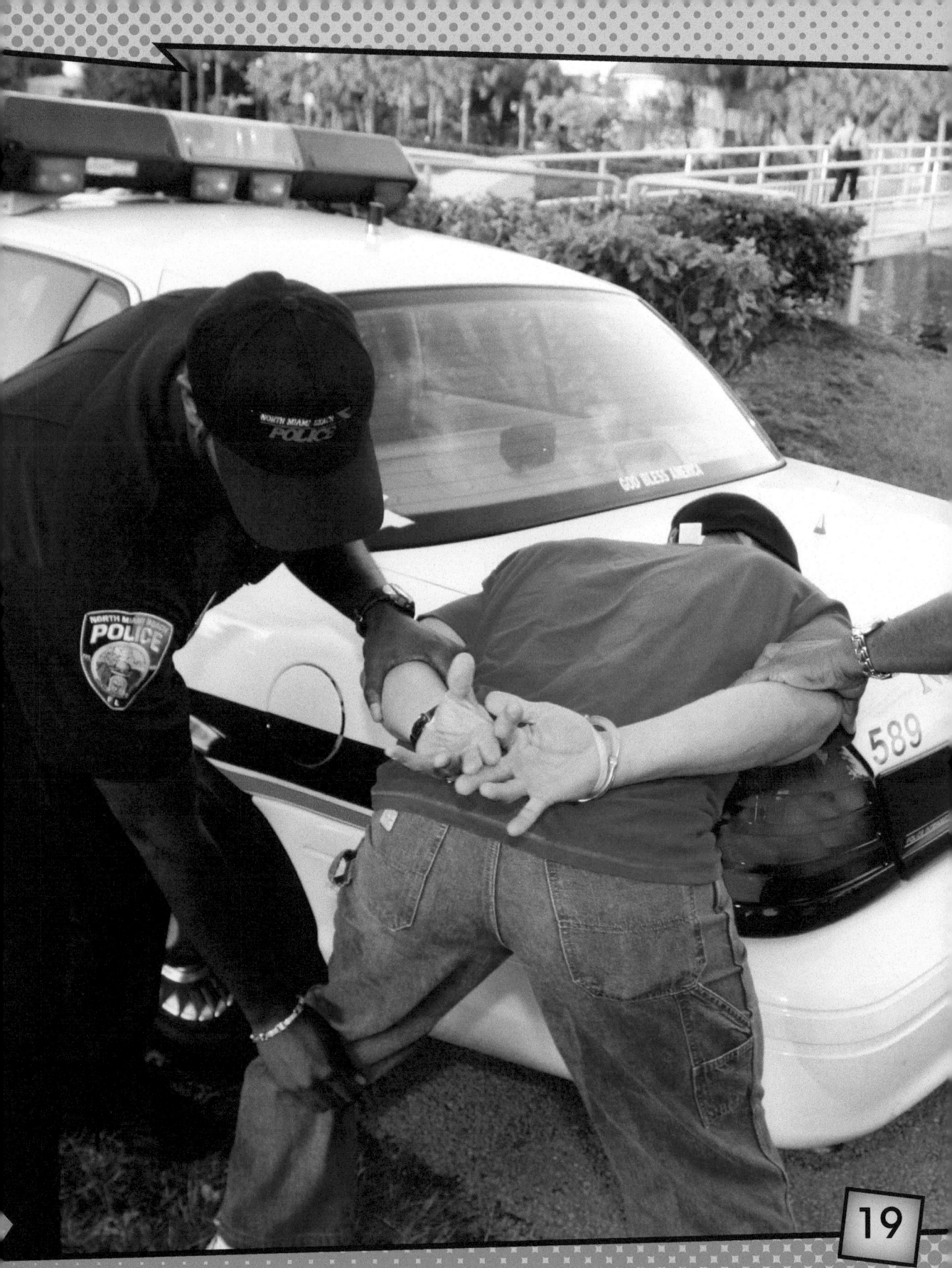
NORTH MIAMI BEACH
POLICE
GOD BLESS AMERICA
NORTH MIAMI BEACH
POLICE
589

Stolen Goods

Some police raids are to recover stolen goods. In a raid near Sydney, Australia, in January 2009, police discovered the country's biggest shoplifting crime ever. A large warehouse was filled with stolen makeup, perfumes, razor blades, and shampoos. The total value of the **loot** was millions of dollars.

Did you know?
Some stolen paintings can be worth millions of dollars.

Escape!

Sometimes, a suspected criminal escapes in a car during a police raid. The police drive after the suspect. Police helicopters also fly above the cars. They tell the officers in the police cars which way the **suspect** is driving.

Did you know?
Police sometimes put down spike strips on the road ahead of a suspect's car. These burst the suspect's car tires.

Caught in the Act

Sometimes, the police will get some secret information, or a **tip-off**, to tell them that a crime is going to take place. They set up **surveillance**, or keep watch, at the place where the suspected crime is supposed to happen. Then, they can catch the criminals red-handed!

Becoming a Police Officer

You need to be brave to become a police officer. You will need to train at a police training center, as well as pass written and spoken tests. Police officers should be smart and fit. They are the world's real superheroes. They are crime fighters!

Stay Safe

In an emergency, call for help. It is important to give as much information about the emergency as possible. Never ever make **hoax** 911 calls. It could cost lives. When someone has called 911, emergency help will soon be at the scene.

Did you know?

There are different emergency telephone numbers around the world:

- United States: 911
- Australia: 000
- most of Europe: 112
- UK: 999

Glossary

arrest catch someone and charge them with a crime

detect discover or catch

evidence something found that can prove or disprove that a crime took place

hoax trick, where someone says something has happened, but they are not telling the truth

illegally do something that is against the law

interrogate ask questions in a serious manner

investigate try to find out the truth about something

lookout person who watches for danger

loot stolen goods or money

prevent stop from happening

resist try to stop something from happening

surveillance watch kept over a person

suspect someone who is thought to have done something wrong

tip-off piece of private or secret information

witness somone who sees an event, such as a crime, happening and can tell other people about it

Find Out More

Books

Enz, Tammy. *Beyond the Bars: Exploring the Secrets of a Police Station*. Mankato, Minn.: Capstone Press, 2010.

Miller, Connie Colwell. *SWAT Teams: Armed and Ready*. Mankato, Minn.: Capstone Press, 2008.

Watson, Stephanie. *A Career as a Police Officer*. New York: Rosen Classroom, 2010.

Websites

www.billtheburglar.org
This website has tips on ways to secure your home against burglars.

www.bls.gov/k12/law01.htm
This website has lots of information about what it's like to work as a police officer.

www.police.vic.gov.au/content.asp?Document_ID=12260
This website about a police force in Australia is packed with interesting facts about the police and fun activities.

Index

bulletproof vest 16

criminal 4

drugs 18

emergency 28
evidence 6, 10, 13
explosives 14

helicopters 22

interrogate 10
investigation 10

lookouts 12

radio 16
raid 4, 6, 7, 10, 12, 14, 15, 16, 20

spike strips 23
surveillance 24
suspects 6, 12, 14, 16, 17, 22, 23

taser gun 17
training 26

weapons 15
witnesses 10